Searchlight Books™

World Traveler

Travel to Madagascar

Matt Doeden

Lerner Publications ◆ Minneapolis

Content consultant: Dr. Abdulai Iddrisu, Director, Africa and the African Diaspora Program, St. Olaf College.

Lerner Publications Company
An imprint of Lerner Publishing Group, Inc.
241 First Avenue North
Minneapolis, MN 55401 USA

For reading levels and more information, look up this title at www.lernerbooks.com.

Main body text set in Adrianna Regular.
Typeface provided by Chank.

Editor: Brianna Kaiser

Library of Congress Cataloging-in-Publication Data

Names: Doeden, Matt, author.
Title: Travel to Madagascar / Matt Doeden.
Description: Minneapolis : Lerner Publications, [2024] | Series: Searchlight books—world traveler | Includes bibliographical references and index. | Audience: Ages 8–11 | Audience: Grades 4–6 | Summary: "Madagascar is known for its vast plant and animal life, but what else should you know about the country? Learn some amazing facts and discover Madagascar's history, culture, geography, and more in this book"— Provided by publisher.
Identifiers: LCCN 2022036913 (print) | LCCN 2022036914 (ebook) | ISBN 9781728491639 (library binding) | ISBN 9798765600719 (ebook)
Subjects: LCSH: Madagascar—Juvenile literature.
Classification: LCC DT469.M26 D63 2024 (print) | LCC DT469.M26 (ebook) | DDC 969.1—dc23/eng/20220815

LC record available at https://lccn.loc.gov/2022036913
LC ebook record available at https://lccn.loc.gov/2022036914

Manufactured in the United States of America
1-53102-51112-12/19/2022

Table of Contents

Chapter 1

GEOGRAPHY AND CLIMATE

Madagascar is a land of lush forests and diverse wildlife. It's the second-largest island nation in the world. Madagascar lies in the Indian Ocean, off the southeastern coast of Africa. The Mozambique Channel separates Madagascar from the African coast.

Madagascar covers 226,658 square miles (587,041 sq. km), making it the world's fifty-fourth largest country. Its three main geographic regions are the coastal strip, the central plateau, and the western plateau and plains.

The coastal strip lies along eastern Madagascar. It's covered in rain forest. Farther inland is the central plateau. It includes several mountain ranges. The Andringitra Massif is in the south, and the Ankaratra range covers central Madagascar. The Tsaratanana Massif is in the north. It includes Maromokotro, the highest peak in Madagascar at 9,436 feet (2,876 m).

Lower-lying plateaus and plains dominate western Madagascar. Mangrove forests grow along the coastline.

CANAL DES PANGALANES RUNS ALONG MADAGASCAR'S EAST COAST.

Rivers and Lakes

The Mangoky River is the longest river in Madagascar. It flows west about 350 miles (563 km) from the central plateau to the Mozambique Channel. Other major rivers include the Onilahy, Betsiboka, and Sofia.

Lake Alaotra is the largest lake in the country. This shallow lake covers about 350 square miles (906 sq. km) of the central plateau. It's home to a wide variety of wildlife, including the Lac Alaotra gentle lemur and many species of birds.

Madagascar's Mangoky River

STORM CLOUDS GATHER OVER ANTANANARIVO, MADAGASCAR.

Climate

Madagascar has two seasons. A hot, rainy season lasts from November to April. Monsoon winds bring moisture to the island. The heaviest rains fall on the highlands in the central part of the island.

May to October brings a cooler, drier season. Trade winds blow from east to west. Most of the rain falls along the east coast.

Southwestern Madagascar gets less rain than the rest of the island. Much of it has an arid climate.

Tropical cyclones often strike Madagascar. They are most common from December to March. These powerful storms bring high winds, heavy rainfall, and sometimes flooding.

The Andringitra Massif is found in southern Madagascar.

Must-See Stop:
Andasibe-Mantadia National Park

Nature lovers won't want to miss the chance to visit Andasibe-Mantadia National Park in eastern Madagascar. The park is in the center of Madagascar's dense rain forest. Visitors can see the park's famous "singing" indri lemurs, huge Parson's chameleons, butterflies, birds, and more. The park is home to Lemur Island, where rangers care for lemurs that could not survive on their own.

Chapter 2

HISTORY AND GOVERNMENT

Madagascar was once a part of Africa. Over 150 million years ago, it separated from the continent. For much of its history, no people lived on the island.

Early Cultures

No one knows when the first humans settled on Madagascar. But over the last two thousand years, the island has seen several waves of migration, mainly from

Africa and Indonesia. Over time, these groups mixed to create the Malagasy culture.

The early Malagasy people split into smaller ethnic groups. The highlanders lived in central Madagascar. The coastal dwellers stayed along the island's shorelines.

The arrival of people brought changes to Madagascar. The Malagasy cleared forests to make farmland. They hunted many of the island's native species. Giant lemurs, pygmy hippos, and other animals went extinct.

Malagasy people walk through a market in a village near Antsirabe, Madagascar.

New Influences

Around 800 to 900 CE, Arab traders from the Middle East arrived in Madagascar. Explorers from parts of Africa and countries such as India followed. Madagascar became a major trading hub.

In 1500, Portuguese sailor Diogo Dias became the first European confirmed to reach Madagascar. Portuguese settlers soon came to the island. In the 1700s, French settlers arrived. With the rise of explorers, and because of its geographic location, Madagascar

Portuguese sailor Diogo Dias arrived in Madagascar in 1500.

became a base for pirates. It was also a key stopping point in the slave trade. Black Africans were captured and forced into slavery.

Meanwhile, the island's people fought for power. In 1810, Radama I, a Merina king, took control of the island. The Merina people are highlanders in Madagascar. After succeeding his father, Andrianampoinimerina, Radama I united warring factions in the kingdom. He gained support of Great Britain, brought British missionaries to the island, and worked to build up the kingdom's industry.

A painting of the Merina king Radama I

A monument in Antoetra, Madagascar, honors the Malagasy people of the 1947 rebellion.

Uprising and Independence

By 1900, after many years of war with the people, France controlled Madagascar. In March 1947, the people of Madagascar rebelled against France. The fighting lasted two years. The rebellion failed, and about eighty thousand Malagasy people died.

But the rebellion did help bring change. France loosened its hold on the island. In 1958, Madagascar became a self-governing state in the French Community. On June 26, 1960, it became fully independent of France.

For the next six decades, corrupt leadership and political strife held back the nation's economy. Its people suffered as leaders used violence to gain and hold power. From 2001 to 2009, Marc Ravalomanana was president. He promised a return to democracy. He promoted health care and education, giving Madagascar's people a greater sense of hope for the future.

President of Madagascar Andry Rajoelina (*left*) meets with French president Emmanuel Macron in 2019.

Let's Celebrate:

Martyrs' Day

Every year on March 29, the people of Madagascar celebrate Martyrs' Day. It honors the people who died in the Malagasy Uprising of 1947 against French rule. The holiday started as a day to mourn the dead. But it has become a celebration of freedom. People traditionally spend the day with family. They relax, connect with one another, and remember those who gave their lives for Madagascar's independence.

Government

Madagascar is a semi-presidential republic. Its people vote for most of their leaders. The president appoints others, including the prime minister. Together, they lead the executive branch.

The legislative branch makes laws. Madagascar's legislature has two branches, the Senate and the National Assembly. The people vote for members of the National Assembly. Local officials and the president appoint senators. The judicial branch applies the law. It is led by the Supreme Court, the highest court in the land.

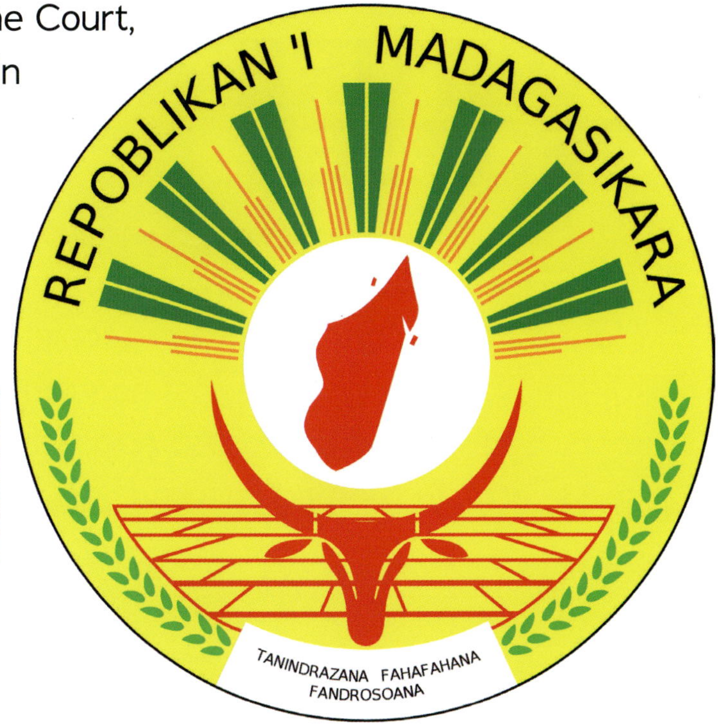

The seal of Madagascar

Chapter 3

CULTURE AND PEOPLE

More than twenty-eight million people live in Madagascar. It's the world's fifty-third most populous country. With roots in Africa and Southeast Asia, Madagascar offers unique arts, music, and culture.

Most of Madagascar's people identify as ethnically Malagasy. The Malagasy are divided into smaller ethnic groups. The largest group is the Merina people, followed by the Betsimisaraka and the Betsileo. Smaller ethnic populations in Madagascar include people of French and Indian descent.

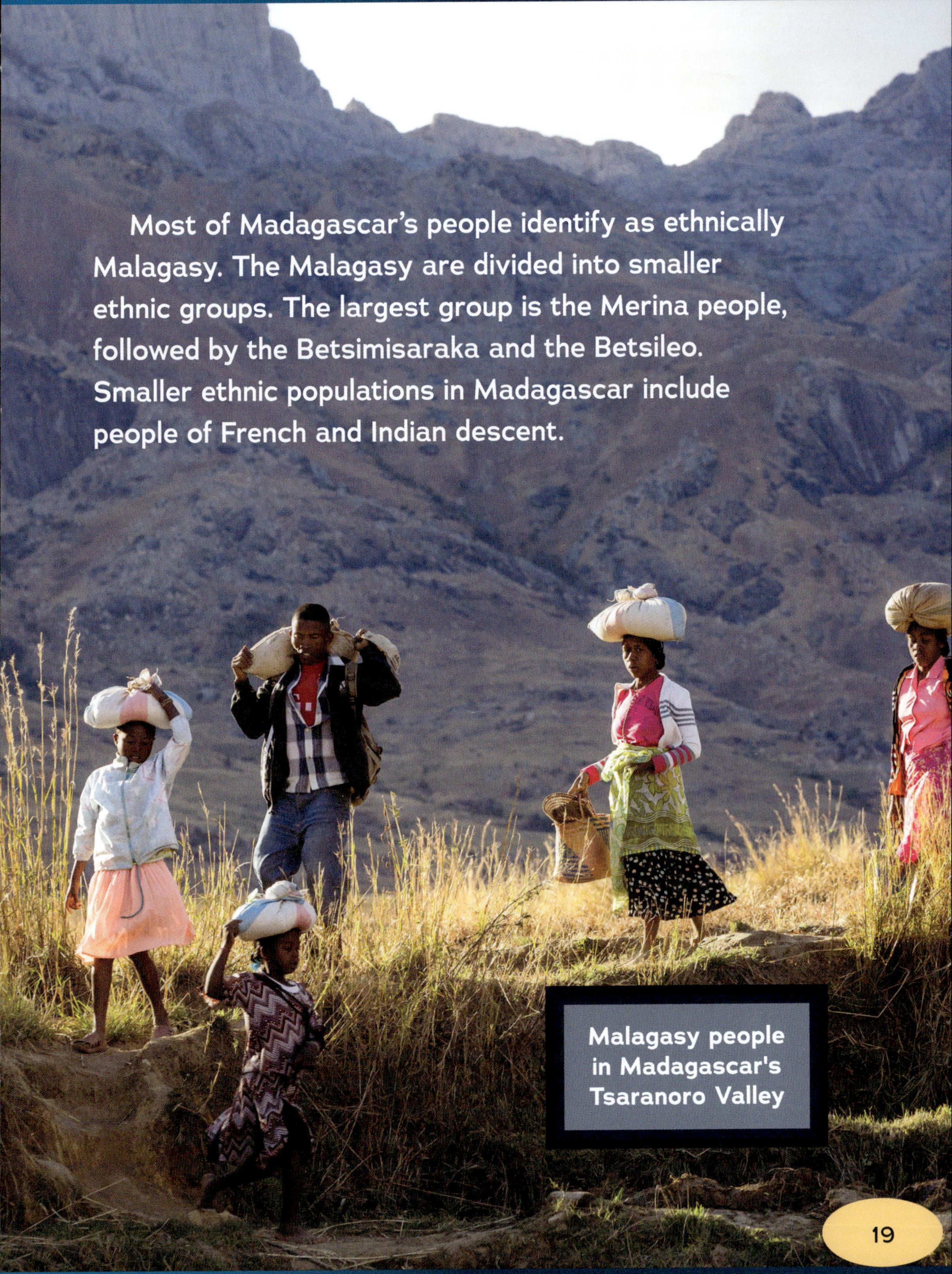

Malagasy people in Madagascar's Tsaranoro Valley

A church in Toamasina, Madagascar

Religion

About 47 percent of Madagascar's people identify as Christian. Missionaries brought the religion to the island after Europeans arrived in the 1500s.

About 42 percent of Madagascar's people follow traditional beliefs. Most traditional belief systems center on ancestor worship. People who follow this faith believe that spirits reward and punish the living for their actions.

About 2 percent of the island's people are Muslims. They follow the Islamic faith and mainly live along the northwest coastline. This religion came to Madagascar with Arab traders. Other people in Madagascar don't identify with a particular faith.

Language and Writing

Malagasy is the official language of Madagascar. Almost everyone speaks it. Malagasy includes elements from Arabic and Africa's Bantu languages. Several dialects of Malagasy exist. The Merina dialect is the most common and the official dialect for Madagascar's government.

Modern Malagasy is written in Latin letters, just as English is. It can also be written in Sorabe script. This alphabet is based on Arabic.

This dictionary translates Malagasy, Madagascar's official language, to French, another language spoken in the country.

Food and Art

Madagascar's cuisine blends flavors and ingredients from Africa, Asia, India, and the Middle East. Rice is the staple of the Malagasy diet. Rice is served with vegetables and meat. Ginger, garlic, curry, and other spices add flavor. Vanilla beans, which grow on the island, flavor many Malagasy desserts, including puddings and cakes.

Madagascar has a rich tradition of arts and crafts. There are sculptures made from the bones of zebu, a kind of cattle, and delicately embroidered fabrics. Music in Madagascar blends tradition with modern styles. It often focuses on family, history, and storytelling.

RICE IS A PART OF MANY DISHES IN MADAGASCAR.

Must-See Stop:

Royal Hill of Ambohimanga

Take a step back in time to see how Malagasy royalty lived hundreds of years ago. Visitors to the Royal Hill of Ambohimanga can see the homes and artifacts of Madagascar's early kings. They can explore the ancient city, see burial grounds, and tour the city walls. The city is sacred to the Malagasy people and remains a place of worship.

Chapter 4

DAILY LIFE

Most of Madagascar's people live in the central highlands or along the east coast. Many live in small towns and villages. Only about 40 percent of its people live in urban areas. Antananarivo is the capital. It's Madagascar's largest city, with almost 1.4 million people. Madagascar's next three most populous cities are Toamasina, Antsirabe, and Fianarantsoa.

A Malagasy person works in a vanilla manufacturing plant in Sambava, Madagascar, in 2017.

About 64 percent of Madagascar's people work in agriculture. They grow rice, vanilla beans, and other crops. About 27 percent work in the service industry with jobs in tourism and communications. About 9 percent work in manufacturing and mining. They create cotton fabric and agricultural goods as well as mine minerals.

Children ages six through thirteen attend school. Many continue beyond that. Almost 80 percent of Madagascar's people can read and write.

Let's Celebrate:
Whale Festival

Each July, people flock to the island of Nosy Boraha, also known as Sainte-Marie, off the eastern coast of Madagascar for the Whale Festival. Thousands of humpback whales come to the island's waters to give birth to calves. The festival kicks off with parades. Visitors enjoy local foods, concerts, and more. The main event is whale watching. Watchers have plenty of photo opportunities as whales breach above the ocean's surface.

CHILDREN ATTEND A PRIMARY SCHOOL IN MADAGASCAR IN 2018.

Future Challenges

Madagascar's population is booming, with a growth rate of about 2.6 percent. That leads to a young population. About three-fourths of Madagascar's people live below the poverty line. They face barriers that make it difficult to meet their basic needs. Madagascar's poverty rate is one of the highest in the world.

Climate change is another major challenge. The rise of global temperatures is having drastic effects. Less rain is falling on Madagascar, and droughts are causing food shortages. With less food and more people, Madagascar faces a crisis. Rising sea levels threaten Madagascar's coastal cities and mangrove forests.

Madagascar is doing what it can to face these challenges. It is trying to slow deforestation in the country. It has worked to reduce its use of fossil fuels. Its people remain hopeful about the future.

Climate change is harming fish habitats around the world, including the waters surrounding Madagascar.

Map and Key Facts

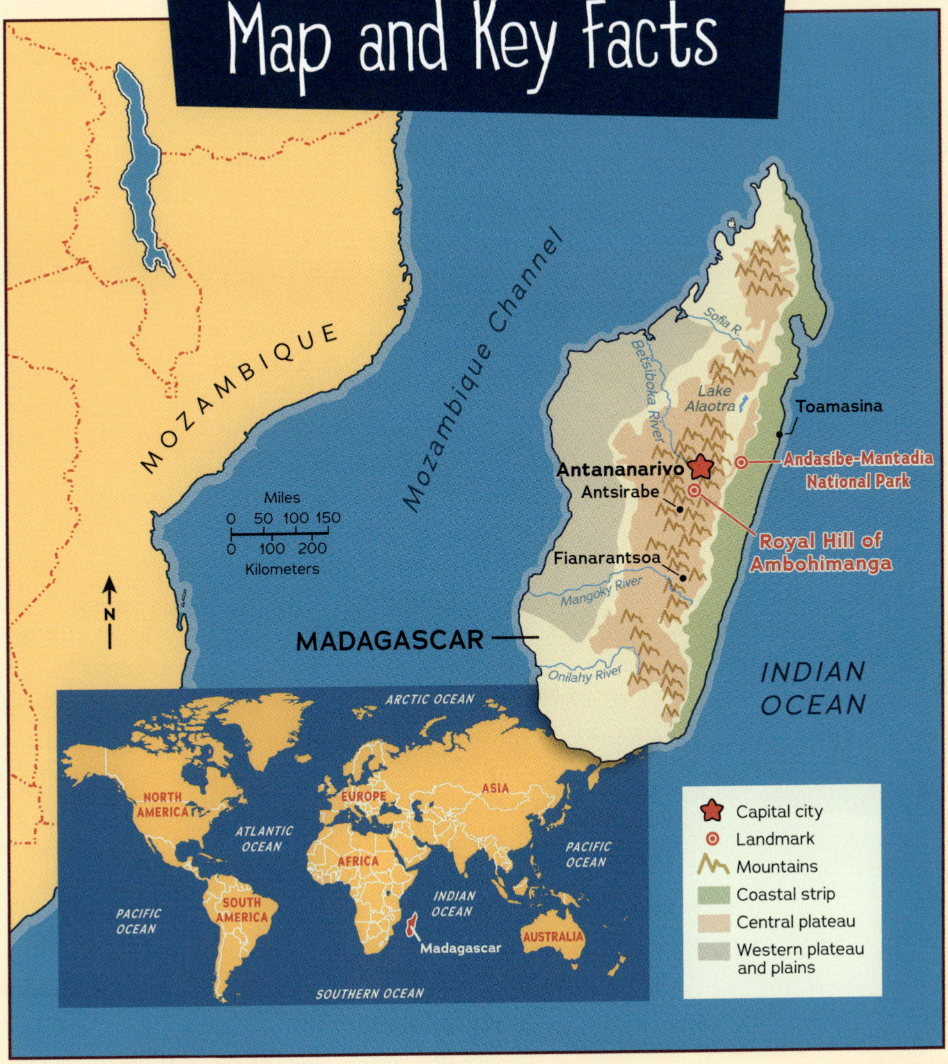

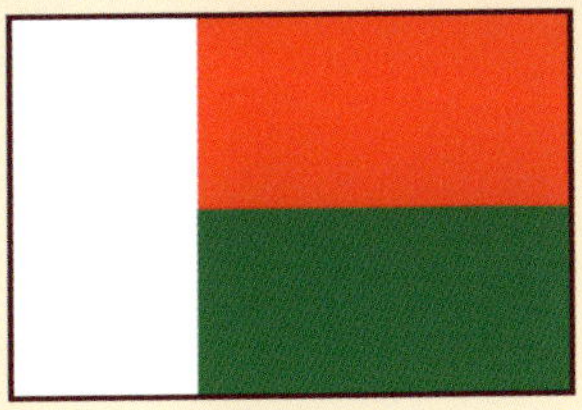

Flag of Madagascar

- **Continent: Africa**
- **Capital city: Antananarivo**
- **Population: 28,172,462**
- **Languages: Malagasy, French, and English**

Glossary

arid: receiving very little rain

cyclone: a strong storm that forms over warm ocean waters, bringing heavy rain and powerful winds

dialect: a version of a language, usually spoken in a specific area

drought: a long period of low rainfall

ethnic: people who share the same race, culture, or nationality

mangrove: a tree that grows in coastal areas that are flooded at high tide

missionary: a person who tries to spread a religion in a foreign land

monsoon: a seasonal wind that brings heavy rains

plateau: an area of high, mostly level land

republic: a government that has elected representatives

Learn More

Golkar, Golriz. *Madagascar.* Minneapolis: Bellwether Media, 2021.

Kerry, Isaac. *Climate Change Migrants.* Minneapolis: Lerner Publications, 2023.

Kids World Travel Guide: Madagascar
https://www.kids-world-travel-guide.com/facts-about-madagascar.html

Madagascar: Treasure Island
https://madagascar-tourisme.com/en/

National Geographic Kids: Madagascar
https://kids.nationalgeographic.com/geography/countries/article/madagascar

Spanier, Kristine. *Madagascar.* Minneapolis: Jump!, 2022.

Index

Photo Acknowledgments

Image credits: Pierre-Yves Babelon/Getty Images, p. 5; robertharding/Alamy Stock Photo, p. 6; mihtiander/Getty Images, p. 7; guenterguni/Getty Images, p. 8; Artush/Getty Images, p. 9; Arterra Picture Library/Alamy Stock Photo, p. 11; CPA Media Pte Ltd/Alamy Stock Photo, p. 12; Philippe-Auguste Ramanankirahina/Wikipedia, p. 13; Hardscarf/Wikipedia, p. 14; Patrick Gely/Pool/ABACAPRESS.COM/Alamy Stock Photo, p. 15; He Xianfeng/Xinhua/Alamy Stock Photo, p. 16; Thommy/Wikipedia, p. 17; mage Professionals GmbH/Alamy Stock Photo, p. 19; robertharding/Alamy Stock Photo, p. 20; Vysotsky/Wikipedia, p. 21; Kieran Stone/Getty Images, p. 22; Jose Antonio/Wikipedia, p. 23; Pierre-Yves Babelon/Shutterstock, p. 25; Conny de Poorter/Alamy Stock Photo, p. 26; RIJASOLO/AFP/Getty Images, p. 27; ANTOINE DEMAISON/AFP/Getty Images, p. 28; User:SKopp/Wikipedia, p. 29; Laura Westlund, p. 29.

Cover: Wolfgang Kaehler/Getty Images.